BRIGHT IDEA BOOKS

YOU CAN WORK IN Publishing

by Marne Ventura

raintree

a Capstone company — publishers for children

Raintree is an imprint of Capstone Global Library Limited, a company incorporated in England and Wales having its registered office at 264 Banbury Road, Oxford, OX2 7DY – Registered company number: 6695582

www.raintree.co.uk
myorders@raintree.co.uk

Edited by Charly Haley
Designed by Becky Daum
Production by Claire Vanden Branden
Originated by Capstone Global Library Ltd
Printed and bound in India

ISBN 978 1 4747 7534 2 (hardback)   ISBN 978 1 4747 7358 4 (paperback)
22 21 20 19 18   22 21 20 19 18
10 9 8 7 6 5 4 3 2 1   10 9 8 7 6 5 4 3 2 1

British Library Cataloguing in Publication Data
A full catalogue record for this book is available from the British Library.

Acknowledgements
We would like to thank the following for permission to reproduce photographs: iStockphoto: Alvarez, 19, Jacob Ammentorp Lund, 12–13, Wavebreakmedia, 5; Shutterstock Images: Dotshock, 30–31, ESB Professional, 6, FXQuadro, 10–11, g-stockstudio, 24–25, GaudiLab, 9, 16–17, Jasminko Ibrakovic, cover, Kdonmuang, 29, Lightfield Studios, 26–27, Monkey Business Images, 6–7, 15, 21, PR Image Factory, 23. Design Elements: iStockphoto, Red Line Editorial, and Shutterstock Images.

CONTENTS

PUBLISHING

Publishers make and sell books. Making a book takes a long time. There are many steps. There are people with different jobs for each step.

Writers write books or stories. **Agents** help writers find **editors**. Editors prepare **text** to be published. They correct mistakes. They make the text the best it can be. **Designers** put text on pages. They might add pictures. They make plans for what books will look like. Finished books are sold by people who work in sales and **marketing**.

Publishers also make magazines, newspapers and other media.

5

People who work in publishing often work together in an office.

Editors like to read. Designers like art. They all work well with others. They are organized. Most have a university degree. Some learn on the job. Would you like a job in publishing?

HOW MANY BOOKS?

In 2015, 173,000 new books were published in the United Kingdom.

People who work in publishing know how to work on more than one thing at a time.

CHAPTER 2

WRITERS

There are many different types of writers. Some write books. Others write for newspapers, magazines or websites.

Fiction writers create stories.

They use their imaginations to write.

They might write mystery books. They
could write adventure stories. They may
write funny stories too.

A writer might take notes on paper before typing a story on a computer.

A writer reads a lot.
He must learn about
the craft of writing.

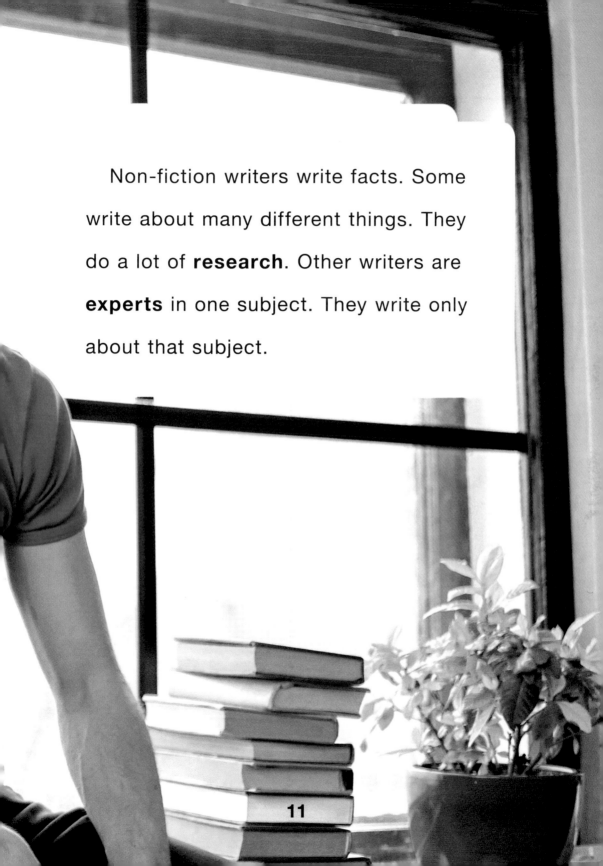

Non-fiction writers write facts. Some write about many different things. They do a lot of **research**. Other writers are **experts** in one subject. They write only about that subject.

A writer does research before writing a non-fiction book.

WRITERS ON THE ROAD

Many writers travel for their jobs. They may travel for research. They may go on a tour to sell their books.

Writers are good with words. Most also enjoy reading. Many writers go to university and study English. Some study a subject they want to write about. They may study maths, art or science. They become an expert in that subject.

CHAPTER 3

AGENTS AND
Editors

Some writers send their work to an agent. Agents know different editors and book publishers. Agents help writers to get their work published.

An agent talks to a lot of people.

15

Editors work with writers. They prepare books and stories to be published. Editors correct grammar. They check facts. They help writers make the text perfect. Editors can work for book publishers, newspapers or magazines.

An editor reads text many times before it's ready to print.

Editors and agents often start out as assistants. They learn on the job. They have great writing skills.

CHAPTER 4

DESIGN

Editors send text to graphic designers. Designers create book covers and page designs. They use computer programs to make the designs.

Designers work with editors. They decide what a book should look like. A children's story might need drawings. A cookbook might need photos. A history book might need maps. A photo researcher finds **images**. Artists and photographers help too.

A graphic designer works to make books look good.

The book has a **deadline**. That is the date when the text and design must be finished. Designers make sure each page looks good. The finished text and designs are sent to a **printer**. The printer turns them into a real book.

Most designers studied art or graphic design at college or university.

An editor and
designer share ideas.

CHAPTER 5

SALES AND
Marketing

Published books need to be sold to readers. People who work in sales and marketing do this. They make plans to sell books.

Someone who works in marketing must be organized.

People who work in marketing often work as a team.

Most people who work in marketing have studied business or marketing.

They might plan advertisements. They find ways to get the books in front of buyers. Salespeople talk to customers. They suggest books to customers.

Do you like reading? Do you enjoy making up stories or researching facts? Or do you think about what books should look like? You might like to work in publishing!

A love of books is important for someone who works in publishing.

27

GLOSSARY

agent
person who does business for someone else

deadline
date that work needs to be done by

designer
person who makes a plan for what something will look like

editor
person who reviews and changes written work to prepare it for print

expert
person who knows a lot about certain subjects

image
illustration or photo

marketing
promoting or selling products

printer
business that makes printed paper items such as books or newspapers

publisher
person or group that prints books or other media

research
studying, usually for a specific project

text
written words

FIND OUT MORE

Interested in publishing? Check out these resources:

Books

Get Writing!, Charlotte Guillain (Raintree, 2014)

Publishing: Books and Magazines (Behind the Scenes), Sarah Medina
   (Wayland, 2013)

Website

nationalcareersservice.direct.gov.uk/job-profiles/publishing-and-journalism
This website tells you about many jobs in publishing. Ask an adult or use a
dictionary to help you understand any difficult words.

ACTIVITY

PUBLISH YOUR OWN BOOK

1. Come up with an idea for a story. Is it a funny story? Is it scary? Is it magical? Maybe it's about something that happened in your life.

2. Write the story. You can do this on a computer or on paper.

3. Edit it. Make sure it reads well!

4. Design the pages and the cover. You can do this on a computer or on paper. Make sure it looks interesting. People should want to read your story!

5. Advertise it. Tell your family or friends. Draw an advertisement and hand it out to people you know.

INDEX